FROM ANXIOUS TO AWESOME

6 PROVEN TOOLS FOR ELIMINATING ANXIETY WITHOUT THERAPY OR MEDICATION

6 PROVEN TOOLS FOR ELIMINATING
ANXIETY WITHOUT THERAPY
OR MEDICATION

CHRIS DINEHART

PLAIN SIGHT PUBLISHING
AN IMPRINT OF CEDAR FORT, INC.
SPRINGVILLE, UTAH

ISBN 13: 978-1-4621-4406-8

Published by Plain Sight Publishing, an imprint of Cedar Fort, Inc.
2373 W. 700 S., Suite 100, Springville, UT 84663
Distributed by Cedar Fort, Inc., www.cedarfort.com

Library of Congress Control Number: 2022946436

Cover design by Courtney Proby

Edited by Michael Morris and Valene Wood
Interior design by Joshua T. Dennis
Illustrations by David A. Green

Printed in Colombia

10 9 8 7 6 5 4 3 2 1

Printed on acid-free paper

Dedicated to my beautiful wife, Emily,
who never stops believing in me

CONTENTS

A NOTE TO THE ANXIOUS

I hope you enjoy reading *From Anxious to Awesome.* All material in this book is provided for informational purposes only. The author sharing this information does not assume any responsibility for the accuracy or outcome of your use of its contents. Every attempt has been made, however, to provide well-researched and up-to-date content at the time of writing.

Before we get started, I want you to keep something in mind. Anxiety is a part of everyone's life. We all face stress, uncertainty, and sticky situations. But with the right tools, most of us can control or even eliminate our anxiety. Most of us can change our lives in ways we never thought possible. But that's not to say this book is all you need if you're suffering from severe, constant anxiety that often leaves you paralyzed. If you have a clinical anxiety disorder—five have been recognized—you should probably seek professional help.

For the rest of you out there anxious to go to battle against anxiety, let's get started.

INTRODUCTION

A popular legend, often attributed to an old Cherokee Indian, tells the story of a grandfather who shared a wise warning with his grandson.

"A fight is going on inside me," he tells his grandson. "It is a terrible fight, and it is between two wolves. One is evil. He is anger, envy, sorrow, regret, greed, arrogance, self-pity, guilt, resentment, inferiority, lies, false pride, superiority, and ego. The other is good. He is joy, peace, love, hope, serenity, humility, kindness, benevolence, empathy, generosity, truth, compassion, and faith."

The grandfather then looks deep into his grandson's eyes and says, "The same fight is going on inside you and inside every other person." The boy ponders for a minute and asks, "Which wolf will win?"

His grandfather answers, "The one you feed."

Which wolf are *you* feeding? Like most people, you are probably not yet the person you truly want to be. As a result, you are not getting everything out of life you want. You deal in your own way with the gap between expectation and reality, but there's something inside you that yearns for more. It's that voice that tells you to carry on in the face of overwhelming adversity. It's that fire and passion to never give up. It tells you to take a risk, give service, and mend that broken relationship.

Unfortunately, you may be like me. For years, I drowned out that voice by listening to a legion of other voices telling me I wasn't enough—that I had peaked, that my ideas weren't good, and that nobody cared. Those voices made me focus on all the bad things that could happen to me. They fed my anxiety. In turn, I fed the evil wolf that blamed my anxiety on genetics, circumstances, other people, my upbringing, and myriad other things.

Thankfully, I discovered principles that challenged the very core of who I believed I was. In this book, I share those principles with you. I'm going to give you some ideas you may not have heard before. I promise that you will find something in this book that will help you increase the quality of your life. I'm going to show you how to live in a new way. I'm going to show you how to *live for more.* I'm going to talk about how we can feed the good wolf instead of the evil wolf.

For a long time, I was feeding the evil wolf but didn't even know it. I faced a tough realization when I discovered that some of my habits and activities were holding me back from the life I wanted. It was natural for me to live in a world where anxiety was just a part of who I was and that there was nothing I could do about it. If I had stayed in that world, you wouldn't be reading this book. It took me 20 years to discover the cure for my social anxiety problems. On the way, I found some good advice and temporary remedies, but it wasn't until I found the long-term solution that my life changed forever. I'm excited to share my journey with you and to help start you on yours!

Additude

1

THE SPELLING BEE

It was just another day in elementary school, but I remember that the playground football game was particularly fun that morning. I returned from recess and took my seat in the third row of our third-grade class. My best friend sat down next to me as the bell rang, and we talked about the pass he threw to me in the end zone on the last play of the game. Our teacher, whom I will call Ms. Jones, walked to the front of the room after making sure we were all back from recess.

"It's time for the spelling bee, kids!" she said. I had never been part of a spelling bee before, so I thought it would be fun. I was confident that my competitive nature would carry me through the first couple of rounds. Ms. Jones asked all of us to stand up. Then she gave each student a word in turn. They were easy words, and the first round was going faster than I thought it would. Finally, it was my turn.

"Spell the word *attitude,*" she said. I started, but my mind went blank. *Attitude is a hard word. Why do I get a hard word when everyone else gets easy words?* "A-D-D-I-T-U-D-E," I said.

Immediately, the class burst into laughter, including my best friend. I was humiliated and felt an overwhelming sense of embarrassment. For the first time in my life, my face felt hot and turned red. Suddenly, I realized that I wasn't as smart as everyone else. I didn't fit in. This realization was a lot for me to deal with, and I never wanted to feel that way again.

The following week I went to Walmart with my mom. I saw a red folder with the word *attitude* printed on the front. I begged my mom to buy me that folder. She was confused. She had bought me a folder only a few weeks before and didn't understand why I wanted another one. I didn't tell her why. I just knew that I didn't ever want to spell the word *attitude* wrong again. Ever!

When I think back to elementary school, my spelling bee experience in third grade is one of the only things I remember. I remember it because it got burned into my brain. That experience, that pain, that suffering changed the way I saw myself and my life. Our lives don't depend on just one event that happens to us, but this event was significant. We all experience events like this in our lives. Some of these events in the past, though we may not realize it, are connected to the anxiety we experience in the present. Our fear, our embarrassment, and our nervousness are all connected to things we have experienced.

For me, for example, shaking someone's hand made me super nervous. I didn't know what to do or say after the handshake. Instead of smiling or just saying, "Nice to me you," I would overanalyze the situation. My behavior was coming from a place of worry. I had unintentionally conditioned my brain to respond that way. Twenty years later, I discovered that it had all started in grade school. Eventually, my brain started figuring it out. I thought, *There's this one thing that's really dangerous and really scary, and it's not a good idea to do it. That one thing is to talk in front of people. Public speaking and being in the spotlight are dangerous. People are going to laugh at you.*

I had more related experiences throughout high school and into adulthood. Eventually, my problem went beyond public speaking. If I said something in private that someone thought was dumb or even funny, I would feel embarrassed. So, my brain started to connect those things as well. I had 20 years of similar experiences that piled up. I was convinced that those connections and feelings of anxiety were just part of who I was and who I was meant to be. I accepted it and at times wore it as a badge of pride. I saw other people who were outgoing, loved to talk to people, and weren't scared to meet new people or ask women on dates. I thought, *But that's just not me because being outgoing is scary.*

What I didn't realize is that I had built that paradigm. I had personally constructed that personality for myself, and my breathing, my physiology, my posture, my eye movement, and my brain chemistry all supported what I had built.

With that personal story in mind, I am now going to give you the secret to eliminating anxiety. This secret is the first of six tools. Tools 2 through 6 are worthless without Tool 1. This first tool is the big one, the granddaddy of them all! It's the one that makes eliminating anxiety possible. It's the secret to succeeding in making other life changes as well. I know because I have used it to make incredibly empowering and impactful changes in my life. I always start with it.

TOOL 1: THE SECRET

The secret to getting rid of all your anxious baggage is beliefs. Now, I know that sounds simple. Like, okay, if I just believe it's going to happen, it's going to happen, right? It sounds so fluffy and good that you could parade around with it on a T-shirt or post it on Facebook, where you'd get 10,000 likes because everyone would agree with it. Believing has been the message of marketing teams since biblical times, but I'm going to show you how you build beliefs, how you've already built them, and how you can crush old beliefs and build new ones. Why don't we put that on a T-shirt? Too wordy?

Beliefs about ourselves are made up of a different things. Think of beliefs as a table. The top of the table is the belief, and the legs under the table are the evidence that supports that belief.

At some point, our beliefs about ourselves or certain events in our lives get tested. Our beliefs won't stand without enough evidence to support them. We use four types of evidence to create beliefs. Let's explore each type.

Peers

Some of the legs under our belief table can be created by our peers. All it may take is for a coworker or a sibling or a friend to say or do something. For example, let's say you want to try the Keto diet and your sister says, "Oh, no, you shouldn't do that. It doesn't work. It's like starving yourself, and it's not sustainable or healthful. I tried it, and it was the worst thing ever."

You immediately start to create a table leg as you think, "Well, I respect my sister. If her experience with Keto was bad and it didn't work, then it probably won't work for me either. So, it's probably not a good idea. If anyone asks why I'm not doing it, I'll give the same reasons she gave me." Your peers provide evidence for you to think like them.

Environment

We're all born into a different environment. We may create beliefs about ourselves and our worth based on that environment. Environment can include a lot of things—usually things we don't choose and can't control. These are things that would be there even if we weren't. These things can shape who we believe we are and what we believe we can achieve. For example, a person born into a family with lots of money might create prideful beliefs about himself when he compares himself to others. In contrast, a person born into a poor family might develop discouraging beliefs about herself and her value.

This isn't a perfect science, of course. Not all rich people are prideful, and not all poor people undervalue themselves. Rich people who avoid pride and poor people who know their true value don't build undesirable and false beliefs about themselves based on their environment. Instead, they modify their environment to help build empowering beliefs.

Role Models

Role models also affect our beliefs. Our first role models are our parents. From the time we're children, we strive to be just like Mom and Dad. If for some reason we become upset with our parents, we try to be the opposite of them. They're still our role models; we just react to them differently. Other role models could include teachers, religious leaders, mentors, coaches, athletes, movie stars, or other famous people. The reason celebrity endorsements are so powerful is that an endorsement can create a belief about a product out of thin air. Lebron James gets into a car, and we think, *Oh, this model of car must be awesome.* We respect role models who have credibility, so their opinion affects what we believe about ourselves and what we believe about the world.

Events

Events are the last thing that create legs under our belief table. They are often the strongest legs under that table because they usually include emotion. For my social anxiety and me, the spelling bee was an event. That event affected who I believed I was and what I believed about myself. I was only nine years old, but I made one of the biggest decisions of my life. For twenty years after that event, I let nine-year-old Chris run the show. Isn't that crazy! A few years later, while I was in a high school class, a teacher was calling roll. When he got to my name, my voice cracked when I said, "Here." Some of the football players in the class thought that was just hilarious. So, I had another event that made me anxious to speak in front of people or to be in the spotlight.

That's how we create beliefs. The more evidence we have that supports our beliefs about ourselves, the stronger they are. Let's shift gears now and walk through how we build beliefs using our evidence. This is called the belief cycle. It has four steps.

THE BELIEF CYCLE

Step 1: Thought

When I misspelled that word in the third grade, some thoughts came to my mind. Namely, speaking in front of people and being in the spotlight is dangerous. It's also embarrassing, humiliating, and risky. When you're about to use evidence to support a belief, you start with thought. Thoughts lead to beliefs, and beliefs lead to action—or, in my case, inaction.

Step 2: Action

From that miserable moment in the spelling bee on, I didn't want to raise my hand in class, I didn't want to speak in front of the class, and I didn't want to be in the spotlight. I was terrified that I was going to randomly get picked to answer a question and not know the answer. Whenever the teacher did call on me, I became scared. My heart rate rose, my breathing increased, my face turned red, and my mind went blank. I had one goal at school—escape embarrassment. So, the action I took after the spelling bee was not to participate. I didn't do anything except try to hide from the teacher. I didn't make eye contact when she asked questions. I didn't volunteer answers. What I did do was go to great lengths to prevent myself from feeling embarrassed. Those actions got me to the next step in the belief cycle: results.

Step 3: Results

The result I got when I effectively hid from the teacher, took no action, and stayed out of the spotlight was that I avoided pain and embarrassment. For me, that result proved positive. I told myself, "Hey, I'm avoiding pain, I'm avoiding embarrassment, and I fit in again, right?" What's interesting is that my anxiousness in the moment never went away, and I didn't view that anxiousness as the pain to be avoided. I didn't understand that the feeling of anxiousness *was* pain and suffering in and of itself.

That pain and suffering continued throughout elementary school and into high school. I felt anxious every day in every class whether I got called on or not. I was already nervous, I was already scared, I was already freaking out just sitting in my chair hoping I wouldn't be called on. I was thinking, *I just need to avoid pain and embarrassment at all costs.* I got really good at getting that result, which led me to the last step in the belief cycle: creation of the belief.

Step 4: Belief Creation

Once I started getting the results I wanted, it was easy for me to justify my actions by assuming an identity. "I'm a shy person," I would tell myself. "I'm an introvert. I don't like the spotlight. I don't like to speak in front of people. I don't like to dance or sing or do anything in public that could prove embarrassing. I'm just not that person, and I never will be. There's nothing wrong with me.

There are lots of other people like me out there. I've been this way for as long as I can remember. It came naturally."

I accepted the belief that I was shy, reserved, and introverted because I had gathered enough evidence and gone through the cycle over and over. Each time I went through the cycle, I would strengthen my belief. I remember hearing my mother tell another adult that I was a quiet boy. Bam! Role model opinion pushed me through the belief cycle in an instant. I made a new friend who was shy and reserved. He wanted to hang out with just me because we were both shy. Bam! Peer opinion instantly pushed me through the belief cycle.

I hope you can see how we start to create beliefs about ourselves and how doing so relates to anxiousness. Let's look at each of the evidence categories and answer some questions so you can relate this cycle to your own life. Grab a pen and write your answers and thoughts to the following questions:

- Peers: Do your peers also suffer from anxiety? How does anxiety help you bond with your peers? What do you believe about anxiety as a result of the influence of your peers?

____

____

____

____

____

- Environment: What things affect your anxiety that you feel are out of your control? What situation were you born into over which you had no choice? What type of living space and transportation do you have? Does either contribute to your stress?

____

____

____

____

____

• Role Models: Whom do you look up to, and what does that person think about anxiety? What have your parents, friends, or religious leaders said about your anxiety? How has your opinion changed based on information given to you by your role models?

____

____

____

____

____

• Events: What events in your life have contributed to your anxiety? What events have been burned into your memory because they were painful or embarrassing? Did you have a third-grade spelling bee experience?

Now we know how to build beliefs and how we've already built them in our lives. It's time for the good stuff. Let's discuss how to crush old beliefs.

THE EXPERIMENT

Back in the 1950s, Dr. Henry K. Beecher of Harvard Medical School was credited with a groundbreaking discovery regarding beliefs. Dr. Beecher, known for his work on the placebo effect, asked 100 medical students to participate in a test of two new drugs. Students were told that the drug in a red capsule was an amphetamine. Amphetamines, or "uppers," create feelings of energy, wakefulness, excitement, attentiveness, concentration, and euphoria. Students were also told that the drug in a blue capsule was a barbiturate. Barbiturates, or "downers," create feelings of relaxation, reduced inhibition, and sedation. When the students were asked about the effectiveness of the drugs, the majority reported experiencing effects consistent with each drug's respective description.

What Dr. Beecher did not tell students was that the drugs had been switched. The red capsule was actually the barbiturate, and the blue capsule was actually the amphetamine. The study showed that the power of the students' beliefs was enough to override the chemical effect of the drug and produce the opposite results. Dr. Beecher said that a drug's usefulness "is a direct result of not only the chemical properties of the drug, but also of the patient's belief in the usefulness and effectiveness of the drug" (in Anthony Robbins, *Awaken the Giant Within* [Simon & Schuster, 1991], 76–77).

I love this story, but when I heard it, I thought it was made up. I was like, "Yeah, whatever. What part of the experiment are you not telling me?" I had to look it up. Turns out it's the real deal. When I learned this, I thought about my social anxiety. I realized that I had never truly believed that I could live without it. I was told—and convinced myself—that being socially anxious was just who I was. It was part of my personality, not something I could control. It just happened naturally. If that wasn't true, then who was I? Who was the real Chris Dinehart? This line of questioning led me to the secret of crushing old beliefs and creating new ones.

CRUSH IT

I had a friend who regularly suffered from anxiety and depression. She had seen a coach and been to a therapist, and she had tried different prescription medications. Nothing seemed to work. Part of her problem was that she had been told over and over that her condition was genetic. Her parents and siblings all suffered from similar symptoms, and they had also been told that their condition was genetic. I can't argue about whether anxiety and depression are in fact genetic. I'm not a geneticist, a licensed therapist, or a psychiatrist. What I can tell you, though, is that your beliefs about yourself and your circumstances will dictate your results.

I sat down with my friend and asked her if she believed she could ever overcome her excessive anxiety. Sadly, she answered no. At that moment, I knew that all the drugs, therapy, and coaching in the world would not be enough to rid her of her suffering. So, I walked her through the same three-step process I stumbled upon in my own life on how to crush a powerful limiting belief.

Step 1: Question It

The first step to crushing a limiting belief is to question it. We spend every day consistently behaving and thinking in accordance with who we believe we are. I realized that I had to start asking myself better questions, and I asked my friend to do so as well. Here are the questions I asked:

- What if I could get rid of this?
- What if there were a way for me not to suffer anymore?
- What if I could overcome the odds?
- What if I could have something different in my life than what I currently have?

Step 2: Envision a New Belief

The second step is to envision what life would be like if you achieved your ultimate goal. I started to envision a Chris Dinehart who was free of social anxiety. This alternate identity looked like me and sounded like me, and he had the same family, friends, and job. But he was a better version of me. I called this guy Chris 2.0. I started to ask some good questions about this alternate identity as I envisioned this person I wanted to become. I asked:

- Who would I be if I didn't have anxiety?
- What habits does Chris 2.0's have?
- How is Chris 2.0 a better husband, father, co-worker, boss, subordinate, team member, leader, and friend?

- What is Chris 2.0 extremely good at now that he's free?
- How does Chris 2.0 make an impact on others because of his victory?
- How does Chris 2.0 feel about himself and others?
- What is Chris 2.0's ultimate goal in life?
- How will Chris 2.0 contribute to the world?
- How does Chris 2.0 deal with fear, anxiety, and embarrassment?
- How does Chris 2.0 respond to difficulty?
- What else does Chris 2.0 do differently?

After answering these questions, I discovered the person I wanted to become. But more important, I started to believe I could find a way to become Chris 2.0. When I did this exercise with my friend, envisioning our new selves, the results were incredible. In just three weeks, she made more progress than she had made after years of therapy and prescription medication. It wasn't because therapy and medication were necessarily bad; it was because she didn't believe they would work. The cruel reality is that disempowering beliefs become self-fulfilling prophecy.

Step 3: Reinforce the Vision

Once you've envisioned a better you, a better tomorrow, a better life, you can take the next step of intentionally connecting with that vision every day. It didn't take me long, however, to discover that envisioning a better version of myself wasn't the end of my journey. I still had days full of fear, discouragement, and embarrassment. I wanted to get rid of social anxiety, but I kept coming face-to-face with past fears that would prompt me to use the same old justifications for giving in. So, I decided to try something.

Every day, I wanted to connect with the vision I had created for myself. To help me, I developed a belief phrase and stated it out

loud every day. I put in on my bathroom mirror. I put in on my desk at work. I put it on a note in my car, displaying it so I'd see it on my way to work every morning and on my commute home every evening. The phrase was, "I got this." Likewise, there is a word or phrase somewhere in your head, something that you have heard that really speaks to you. I call it a power word or a power phrase. Maybe you saw it in a movie or heard it in a song, or maybe you saw it on a plaque or on social media.

Power phrases evoke a deep emotional reaction. You know you've found one when you can't help but get pumped up when you say it out loud. I used my power phrase every time I felt those old habits creeping back into my life. I'd say it three times in the morning right after waking up and three times at night before I went to bed. At the time, I didn't see the long-term effect this activity would have on me. But later, I discovered that I was conditioning my brain to respond with powerful optimism anytime I was presented with something that previously would have caused me to feel anxious. My mind and body instinctively started to create optimism and excitement instead of fear and discouragement.

Go ahead and try it. Choose your power phrase. Then say it out loud every day three times in the morning and three times in the evening.

2

THE BOY WHO CRIED WOLF

"I'm really going to lose the weight this time," I told my wife. "This time, it's going to work." I was embarking on another attempt to shed some pounds, and I was again telling my wife my goal for accountability. "Okay," she said as she gave me a doubtful smile. She had always been supportive, and this occasion was no different. She wanted me to succeed. She offered to make meals that supported my new diet. I knew she would provide motivation for me to achieve my goal. I knew because at this point I had told her upward of thirty times that I was going to start a diet and lose weight.

I didn't know at that moment what she was really thinking, but I couldn't help but feel like the boy who cried wolf. The classic story of the boy who raised false alarm after false alarm to the point that nobody believed what he said when he raised an alarm of real danger. I couldn't help but question myself. Why was losing weight so hard? Was it really worth the effort? Why did it seem to come so easy for everyone else? What if I kept trying but ultimately failed? What if I never changed and suffered disappointment forever?

I really wanted to lose weight, but treats just seemed to taste better than it felt to be fit. Not being able to change myself became another thing that contributed to my anxiety. I didn't like the way I looked or the way I felt, and I feared that people were constantly judging me. I wanted more for myself, and I believed in my potential enough that I was willing to keep trying. But that voice of doubt in my head wouldn't shut up. It had the best excuses, and it knew every little thing about me. It used my weaknesses against me at will. That all changed, however, when I discovered the secret to making *real decisions.* Real decisions lead to incredible results—like my resulting weight loss. I lost the weight and am happy to say that I've kept it off.

TOOL 2: REAL DECISIONS

After I stumbled upon the tool to making real decisions, I found out that successful people already knew and used it. Before, I was a good decision-maker and generally accomplished what I wanted to accomplish. To achieve something great, however, I needed more than that. Let's talk about a few people who have understood this tool and used it effectively to accomplish great things.

Michael Jordan

We all know the story of Michael Jordan not making the varsity basketball team at his high school as a sophomore. From that moment on, he decided what he was going to accomplish: he wanted to become the best basketball player to ever play the game. As a result, he accomplished things that many thought impossible. He thought differently, played differently, and raised the bar for professional athletic training as a result of his decision to accomplish his goal.

Walt Disney

Legend has it that when Walt Disney wanted to build Disneyland in California, his request for financing was rejected 302 times. He had to go to 303 banks and financial institutions before he finally achieved success. I don't know about you, but 302 rejections would definitely cause me to question my beliefs about an idea. Think about that. If 302 businesses rejected your idea and refused to become your financial partner, you would probably give up—especially if you repeatedly heard that your idea was a bad investment. For most of us, a few rejections would cause us to quit.

Colonel Sanders

Both Walt Disney and Michael Jordan had big dreams—dreams of accomplishing somthing grandiose. Colonel Sanders just wanted to sell a little chicken prepared with his chicken recipe. The crazy thing is, nobody wanted it. He was rejected by 1,009 restaurants before one finally agreed to cook and sell his chicken. Again, I don't know about you, but if 1,009 people told me that they didn't want to buy my chicken recipe, I might start thinking about selling hamburgers. Maybe all my friends were lying to me about how good my recipe was, and they just wanted me to feel good about it. Focus on the word *resolve* as you read this quote by Colonel Sanders: "I made a resolve then that I was going to amount to something if I could, and no hours, nor amount of labor, nor amount of money would deter me from giving the best that there was in me."

Hernán Cortés

I want to tell you about one more resolution, which comes from one of my favorite stories. It's about a Spaniard named Hernán Cortés. He came to the New World, the Americas, with 500 men aboard his ships. When he arrived, the first thing he did was unload everybody and then burn the boats, though some accounts say he merely "scuttled" them. Regardless, his goal was to conquer the New World. He sent a message to his men and to himself that he would accomplish his goal at all costs. Destroying the boats was a reminder of that decision. What he didn't know was that he was going to have to fight hundreds of thousands of Aztecs, but it didn't matter. He destroyed the boats because he had decided that he was going to stop at nothing to conquer the Americas. To him, it was achieve it or die.

As for me, I would have probably saved one of the boats—just in case. But Hernán Cortés knew what a *real decision* was—what it meant and what it cost. So did Colonel Sanders, Walt Disney, and Michael Jordan. When I tried to lose weight, I had to learn through trial and error how to make real decisions. I'm sharing my experience because you need to know that you don't give up after one or five or 1,009 rejections or failures. Overcoming anxiety, losing weight, or making other significant changes inevitably requires struggle, but struggle won't cause you to quit if you have made a real decision.

THE ANATOMY OF A REAL DECISION

Requirement No. 1: You've Got Time

If you're going to get rid of anxiety, your timeline for achieving that goal should be infinite. That means that no matter how long it takes, you *will* accomplish it. I am not suggesting that you don't set goals to get there. Goals are an important part of gauging your progress and pushing yourself to achieve something. I am suggesting, however, that if you don't reach a goal, or if you feel discouraged, or if you don't seem to be making progress, then remind yourself that you've already made your decision and you're not turning back. You won't know exactly how long it will to take to get there, and neither did I. But because I had finally made a real decision, losing weight happened a lot faster than I thought it would.

Requirement No. 2: Do Not Bow to the Wind

The next thing a real decision requires is tenacity in the face of any unforeseen circumstance or challenge. Had Hernán Cortés changed his mind after destroying his boats, he likely would have said, "Oh, dang, there are 200,000 Aztecs, and I only have 500 men. I better build some new boats." But he didn't. You can't let your decision succumb to unforeseen adversity.

Let's say you're making progress, but something comes up. You suffer a financial loss, you get fired, your car breaks down, your dog dies. It would be natural to think, "Now I have a bigger reason to feel anxious. Now I have a bigger reason to feel grief. Maybe I'll just put on hold all those things Chris told me to do so I can deal with this."

That won't work if you're serious about eliminating anxiety from your life. No matter what unforeseen challenge or adversity you face, you must continue to be dedicated to your decision. Dedication will make you stronger and more capable of getting through your challenges. You'll have setbacks., of course. You're not going to be perfect. Heaven knows I wasn't. But do everything in your power not to give up—ever.

Requirement No. 3: Do Something

Real decisions are followed by action. If you make a decision and then do nothing, you didn't make a real decision. Decisions don't sound anything like this: "Yeah, it would be nice not to feel anxiety anymore. It would be nice not to be depressed." Such statements sounds like weak pleas for divine intervention. If you keep doing what you're doing, you'll keep getting what you're getting. If you want something different, you have to do something different. You've got to take action.

Requirement No. 4: Set a New Standard

Real decisions set a new standard for acceptable behavior. When you make a real decision, there's a good chance you will have to change your lifestyle. When it comes to ridding yourself of anxiety, you will definitely have to change some of your habits and behaviors. Certain things will no longer be acceptable. I know I had to make changes. At first, it hurt to let go, but the sacrifice was worth it. I started with some small things, like keeping my work, living, and transportation spaces clean. Set a new standard for the type of behavior you will need to have. I assure you that the hardship you go through to make that change will serve as a catalyst to help you on your journey.

Requirement No. 5: Make It Specific and Compelling

To be real, a decision must be specific and compelling. You can't just say, "Oh, yeah, I'm going to get rid of my anxiety." Maybe that's compelling, but it's not specific enough. Ask yourself, "How often is it acceptable for me to feel anxious in a week?" Zero times? Five times? That's a little more specific. "How many Cokes will I allow myself to drink this week?" Two a day? One every other day? Decide on a specific action plan for the short term as well as a broader plan for the long term.

Requirement No. 6: Plan B's Are a Distraction

Just like Hernán Cortés when he "scuttled" his boats, you have no plan B. There's no other option. You will achieve your goal, and you will not be denied. You can change your approach and you can change your strategy, but you're not going to change your plan. Your plan is still to control your anxiety or lose weight or alter some behavior. After I decided to lose weight, I tried a bunch of different diets and exercise routines. Most of them didn't work for me, so I kept changing my approach. Eventually, I found something that worked because I stuck with it. My goal was always a long-term, compelling, and specific outcome. I had no plan B.

In his book *The Greatest Salesman in the World* (1968), Og Mandino wrote, "I will persist until I succeed. I was not delivered unto this world in defeat, nor does failure course in my veins. I am not a sheep waiting to be prodded by my shepherd. I am a lion and I refuse to talk, to walk, to sleep with the sheep. . . . I will persist until I succeed."

There are things you need to do every day in order to reinforce your decision to control your anxiety. Start by setting a specific goal. Write it down. Put it where you can see it every day. It sounds simple, but I know from experience that seeing your goal wakes up your subconscious to what you're going to achieve. Put it in your car, on your bathroom mirror, on your bedroom wall—wherever you'll see it every day. Underneath your goal, write, "I will make this work. I will not be denied. I will persist until I succeed!" Each time you see your goal, say it out loud. When you say it out loud every day, you'll start to believe it. And it will push you to make change happen in your life.

3

ROCKY BALBOA

Rocky Balboa runs through the streets. Being a famous boxer, he doesn't take long to gather a following as people join him on his run. After extended sprints and hurdles, he finally reaches the Philadelphia Museum of Art. He runs to the top of the steps, immediately puts his hands above his head, and jumps up and down, celebrating. The thing is, he hasn't fought anybody yet. Rocky is a boxer, and he's about to go up against the world heavyweight champion, the best fighter in the world. For some reason, this scene takes place while Rocky is training to fight. He celebrates as if he'd already won. *Rocky* is a beautiful underdog story.

Tool 3 is about pairing pain and pleasure to different things in life. I came to the realization that I had paired pain with speaking in public, meeting people, and attending social events. These things didn't have any pain directly associated with them other than the perceived pain I had assigned them. I want you to think of the things that make you anxious on a daily basis or throughout the week. They are associated with some form of pain. What is that pain? Sometimes it's not a big thing that creates anxiety in our lives; rather, it's a lot of little things that start stacking up. Eventually, they feel like one big problem, when really they aren't.

Think about when you feel your heart rate rise or when you feel really nervous about something. Going back to the third-grade spelling bee, I paired the pain of embarrassment with speaking in public. I paired pain and being in the spotlight. Does that mean that every time I was in the spotlight I was going to feel pain? No, but my body thought that was the case. My psychology had those paired together even though it was a false connection.

TOOL 3: PAIN AND PLEASURE

Recently, I saw what Tony Robbins calls "the pain-pleasure principle" come to life with my daughter. At eight months, she paired the sight of her grandparents with the pain of Mom and Dad being gone. Occasionally, her grandparents would babysit her, which she didn't like. Soon, she made a false connection. Now, when we arrive at her grandparents' house for dinner or to visit, she doesn't want to be held by Grandma or Grandpa because she thinks that means Mom and Dad are about to leave. This is a simple example, but we all connect pain and pleasure to things in our lives. Think about the connections you've made to pain and how those connections could be contributing or creating anxiousness in your life.

When I discovered this tool, I had to find a way to pair pleasure with meeting people, speaking in public, and being in the spotlight. I came up with the idea to do the same thing Rocky did. A chemical reaction occurs in your brain when you celebrate by putting your hands in the air. Blind people, who have never seen anybody celebrate, celebrate by putting their hands above their head. The ensuing chemical reaction increases happiness hormones and decreases cortisol. Cortisol is a stress hormone. Think about that for a second. You have the power to instantly increase your happiness and decrease your stress—no matter where you are or what you're doing.

When I used to speak in front of people, I would get nervous, and my fears would bombard me. My anxiousness would do everything it could to prevent me from speaking. But instead of listening to my fears as I prepared to speak, I began putting my hands above my head, jumping up and down, and acting as if my favorite sports team had just won a championship game. With that same simple act, I could pair pleasure and celebration with meeting somebody, speaking in public, and participating in a meeting. The connection between pleasure and socializing started to become strong, and the old pairing of pain and socializing started to disappear. My brain created a new pattern of enjoying those interactions. That was the beginning of a new way of life for me.

Reprogram Your Mind

I love associating pain with undesirable behavior and associating pleasure with desirable behavior. I did it with anxiety, I did it with diet, and I did it with exercise. I began playing my favorite pump-up song as soon as I finished exercising. I would put my hands above my head, jump up and down, and say "Yes!" three times as I watched myself celebrate in the mirror. It sounds ridiculous, I know. But that's what it took for me to reprogram my brain to enjoy exercise. Before, I really didn't enjoy it. In fact, I loathed it. I felt that it was pointless, I hated the smell of the gym, I didn't like getting tired "for fun," and I felt that people constantly judged me.

As soon as I reprogrammed my mind, though, I was able to go to the gym without any effort. My body craves the gym now. I want to feel that celebration after a good workout, and I don't have to motivate myself or think about it to crave that celebration. It became second nature. I've done the same thing with anxiety. I took the things that used to make me the most anxious and created new, positive connections. You too are only a few connections away from getting rid of your anxiousness.

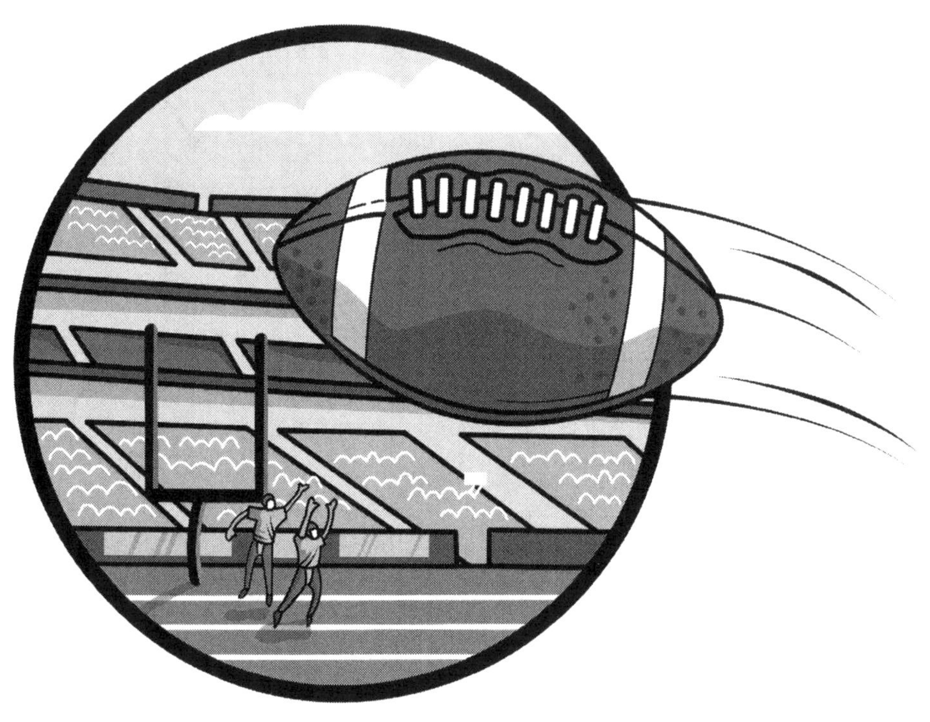

4

THE HAIL MARY

It was fall in Utah. The leaves were changing, and the days was cooling down. It was "the most wonderful time of the year"—football season! I was invited to dinner and a football game at Brigham Young University with the CEO of the company I was working for. We weren't exactly close, and our paths in the office rarely crossed. But we would occasionally exchange the latest articles about BYU football. This was the first time I'd been invited to spend time with the CEO and his wife outside of work parties. He had expensive seats, so my wife and I would be joining him in the exclusive part of the stadium where food was served before each game. To say I was intimidated would be an understatement. I was freaked-out nervous. This was the CEO we're talking about.

When we arrived, we grabbed our food. I didn't say much, though, because I was afraid of saying something wrong. I was also scared that I might drip barbecue sauce on my shirt or spill my drink. That would be just my luck, right? The CEO's wife asked a lot of question questions, to which I gave short, safe replies. Eventually, the table fell silent for some awkward stretches. After what seemed like a never-ending TV time-out, the game finally started. We made our way to our seats in silence and started watching the game. Reserved and rational cheering, with a sprinkle of occasional sports commentating, followed.

As the last minute of the game approached, it became clear that the outcome would come down to one final play. BYU had to score a touchdown. Without a touchdown, the Cougars would lose. I sat nervously as the quarterback dropped back, scrambled under pressure, and then heaved a prayer of a pass, otherwise known as a Hail Mary, into the end zone. By some miracle, the prayer was answered! One of BYU's players hauled in the ball for a game-winning touchdown. In that moment, I went nuts. I let go of all my fear and anxiousness and celebrated like crazy. Likewise the CEO, who was sitting next to me. We screamed as we jumped up and down while double high-fiving. I just let go—let go of all my doubt, fear, and insecurity. I celebrated and enjoyed the moment. My emotional roller-coaster ended on a high note that night.

State of Mind

At the football game, I experienced two different states of mind. That's what I want to talk to you about in order to give you the next tool. What states of mind did I experience? One of them was total insecurity, fear, and doubt. I was feeling really self-conscious, and that created a lot of anxiety. My heart rate was high, and my body language was reserved, shy, and fearful. In stark contrast, at the end of the game, I experienced complete elation, excitement, and happiness. I totally let go of all the other stuff I was experiencing before. The quality of your life is reflected in the quality of your state of mind on any given day. Bad days consist of suffering and pessimism; good days consist of happiness and optimism. Being able to control your state of mind is critical to getting rid of anxiety.

State of Stress

When we feel stressed about something, our heart rate becomes erratic. As the graph below shows, our heart rate bounces up and down and all over the place. There's no consistency. In a mental state of stress, our brain activity also bounces all over the place. It can go really low and then go really high. What's interesting is that our heart rate and our brain waves actually work against each other. When our heart rate is really high, our brain activity is really low. When our heart rate is really low, our brain activity is really high. When they're totally out of sync like this, our body is kind of freaking out, so to speak—all because we're stressed or frustrated or angry or anxious or fearful.

Simultaneously, our ability to make decisions becomes impaired. Studies have shown that our IQ actually drops 10 to 15 points during these moments. Google it. Even the most brilliant minds in the world experience this phenomenon. Smart people act stupid when they're under stress. (See https://arizonaintegrative-hypnotherapy.com/heart-coherence/; accessed Sept. 14, 2023.)

State of Appreciation

In a state of mind of appreciation, our heart rate and our brain waves are in sync, as the graph below shows. They're not only in sync with each other, but they also follow a smooth and consistent pattern. Our mind and body start to function on the same wavelength when we're in a mental state of appreciation.

Being in a high-stress mental state or low-stress mental state, then, can change our behavior. We can all think of moments when we were frustrated and as a result did something we regretted—something we're not particularly proud of. I know I can. On the other hand, I remember moments of gratitude that inspired me to do something really good. Those moments made me want to contribute to someone else's life. To experience more of the beauty of life, we have to live in a beautiful mental state. (See https://www.researchgate.net/publication/232478613_The_Appreciative_Heart_The_Psychophysiology_of_Appreciation; accessed Sept. 23, 2023.)

TOOL 4: PHYSIOLOGY

Now that you know about mental state, it's time to introduce Tool 4. This tool is all about physiology. If you want to get rid of anxiety, you need to use your body. The way you feel physically and emotionally on a daily basis affects your state of mind. At the end of the day, how you feel in those two areas determines the quality of your life. If you feel bad every day, the quality of your life is probably pretty low. Tool 4 is all about showing you how to change in an instant the way you feel, even if you're facing a lot of adversity. If negative things are happening to you, if things are stacking up, and if you start feeling overwhelmed, using your physiology can be an effective tool in helping you snap out of it. Here are some strategies to help you overcome feeling overwhelmed and anxious.

Strategy 1: Celebrate

The first one, which we already talked about, is celebration. People are usually embarrassed to try this one, especially those with social anxiety. If you've ever watched the popular TV show *The Office*, you may have seen the episode where Dwight Schrute uses this tool. Sitting in his car, he celebrates and listens to a pump-up song right before a sales meeting with a potential client. This strategy can provide instant relief if you go all in. Using this strategy, you can quickly exit disempowering states and enter empowering ones. Find something to celebrate, or just celebrate the current moment.

In the movie *Bill and Ted's Bogus Journey* (1991), Bill and Ted say, "The best place to be is here. The best time to be is now." Find something to celebrate every day. If nothing else, celebrate that you are alive and that your heart continues to beat without any effort on your part. I choose to celebrate by jumping up and down with my hands above my head. Do any action you want—whatever comes natural to you.

Strategy 2: Cold Plunges

I do a cold plunge every day. A cold plunge will reassert your psychological control. It's a strategy to get you into an empowering mental state at the beginning of each day. It will also help you understand that *you* are in control. That voice in your head is *not* in control, and you can prove it to yourself every morning with a little help from some cold water.

Here's what I do. First, I take my regular shower and then step out of the water. Then I turn the water dial to as cold as it goes. In that moment, the voice in my head responds, "Hey, don't do this! This is uncomfortable. Why are you doing this? There's no reason to. It's a bad idea. You're just going to freeze. You think something good is going to happen just because you stand in cold water? Are you crazy or stupid?"

That voice rattles off all kinds of rationalizations, but I point to my head and say out loud, "I don't negotiate with you." Then I step into the water and count to 60. I know it sounds dumb. And I know it sounds cold. It is! But let me tell you what it can do for you. Later in the day, when you feel anxious about something and that voice of doubt starts whispering in your ear, you'll remember that you already defied that voice once—and now you can defy it again. Start each day with a victory over that voice, of mind over chatter, and you'll have power to defy that voice throughout the day. As you shut it down, you'll find it easier to control your anxiety. You'll find it easier to focus on your goals. And you'll find it easier to change your mental state from feelings of apprehension to accomplishment.

Strategy 3: Power Poses

Another thing you can do to change your mental state in an instant is to use power poses. Look up the TED Talk by Amy Cuddy in which she talks a lot about power poses and their effects ("Your body language may shape who you are," Oct. 2012). Power poses change your brain chemistry by increasing testosterone, which is associated with aggressiveness and strength. All human beings have testosterone in their bodies. Increasing testosterone levels makes you feel more confident and powerful. The way you stand, sit, or move your body can increase or decrease your testosterone levels. If you walk with your head down and your shoulders slumped, you're going to lower your testosterone and increase your cortisol, which is a stress hormone. If you walk with your chin up, your chest out, and your shoulders back, your body is going to decrease the cortisol in your brain and increase your testosterone.

It sounds simple, but the way you stand can affect whether you feel anxious, depressed, or fearful. So, change the way you sit, change the way you walk, change the way you stand. The Superman pose, with closed fists resting on your hips, is an example of a power pose. Another one, which you can do sitting down, simply requires that you to clasp your hands together, put them behind your head, and point your elbows up. Just leaning back in a chair can be a power posture. Hunching over, having your hands closed or clasped together in front of you, or having your arms folded are weak power poses. Get rid of those. Change the way that you sit, walk, and stand throughout the day and you'll change the chemicals in your brain. Change the chemicals in your brain, and you'll experience less anxiety.

Strategy 4: Music

Music also has power to affect your mental state. For our purposes, I'm not talking about music that makes you feel sad or mad. If there's a song that your old jerk of a boyfriend used to listen to, avoid it. It'll change your mental state for sure, just not to the state we want it to. I don't want you feeling negative emotions. Instead, put together a power playlist—songs that make you feel good and pump you up. Play those songs as often as you can, especially on bad days.

I put on my power playlist when I'm getting ready for the day and even when I'm working my day job. In fact, I'm playing music right now as I work on this book. My playlist is upbeat and exciting, and it makes me feel good. Music can increase your drive, determination, and happiness. Use music to bring back powerful emotions from the past that make you feel good about yourself. When you feel good about yourself, you stack fewer anxious and fearful thoughts on top of each other.

Strategy 5: Dance

Another strategy you should use every day is dance. I discovered this one through personal experience. What's funny is that I had so much social anxiety that I wouldn't fast dance if my wife or anyone else was in a room with me. I could go slow dance with my wife, but dancing to upbeat music was nerve-racking for me. I would fast dance only if I was obligated to.

Dancing is a form of self-expression, and it took a lot for me to let go of my fear and give it a try. Dancing promotes self-confidence and self-expression, and it produces endorphins in your body. Anytime you move your body like a happy, excited person, you produce happiness hormones. It gets hard for discouragement and stress to exist in a body that moves frequently. This insight made a big impact on my ability to change my mental state every day.

Strategy 6: Breathe

Your breathing indicates your mental state. Most of us spend the majority of our lives taking short, shallow breaths. The next time you get excited about something, notice how your breathing changes. I use a breathing exercise that I combine with other activities that we'll discuss in Tool 5. This exercise, called *priming,* was created by Tony Robbins. Look it up on YouTube by searching "Tony Robbins Priming."

In general, breathing exercises can increase the amount of oxygen in your blood. When you have more oxygen in your blood, you're more alert and more mindful of the way your body feels. A breathing exercise can calm your nerves, clear your head of distractions, decrease your cortisol, and increase the endorphins in your body. It can help you get rid of the negative thoughts that the evil wolf feeds you.

THE CHALLENGE

Here is my challenge for Tool 4. It's an action step. In my case, I realized that I was scared of meeting people and of being judged by them. I was scared of what people thought of me. So, I decided that I was going to do something with my body. I decided to give every person I saw a high five. No matter who they were, I was going to give them a high five so that I could face my social anxiety and defeat it head on. I put myself in a position every day—all day long—to do something that challenged my old way of thinking. I started to give everyone a high five. At first, it was tough, but it got easier.

Even if you don't suffer from social anxiety, I challenge you to give everyone you see a high five. It will force you to muster some energy, even on bad days. There's no such thing as a low-energy high five. When I say *everyone,* I mean everyone. Family, friends, the CEO, the person who rings you up at the store—everyone. I felt dumb and awkward so many times, but over the space of a few weeks, I had given so many high fives that I started to stop caring. My mindset and my thoughts started to change. I started asking, "When I give someone a high five, what do I lose?" Some people laugh at me or look at me weird, but at the end of the day, I'm just giving them some happiness.

I traded my anxiety for their happiness. In return, I built an iron-clad and battle-tested confidence in myself. It wasn't long before I wasn't embarrassed to do it anymore. The fear was gone. I stopped caring what other people thought. This challenge changed my life. I know it will change yours if you take it seriously. It will change your mental state into one of confidence and strength. To this day, I don't care if other people judge me, because I love myself. I can't control what others think anyway. They're already thinking it, so why should I stress? Those who feel scared to give high fives will benefit most from giving them. Start giving high fives, and I promise that your fear will eventually go away. Welcome to the #highfiver family.

STRESS
FEAR
WORRY

5

THE RECRUIT

It was a regular day at the office when the president of the company brought a potential recruit in to meet me. I worked in operations and played an integral part in making new recruits feel welcome and to ensure that their integration was smooth. This was a big recruit who could bring a lot of business to the company. I needed to make a good first impression.

I stood up to shake his hand and said, "Hi. It's great to meet you." He told me his name as I overanalyzed my posture, tone of voice, eye contact, and body language. As he spoke, I realized that I had already forgotten his name. I made a mental note to avoid having to say his name. Then I frantically tried to find something to talk about—some type of conversation starter. Anything would be better than nothing. "Just don't say something dumb," I told myself. "That would be embarrassing."

During an awkward pause, I realized he had asked me a question. I didn't hear it. I had been making eye contact and nodding my head as if I were paying attention, but mind had fled to anxious land. *Now what?* I thought. *Oh, no, my face is turning beet red. I can feel it! That will go well with my sweaty armpits and the panic in my eyes. Looks like this might be the last time I ever meet a potential recruit. If I don't get fired, that is. Hide, Chris! Aah!*

Safe to say, we didn't land the recruit.

TOOL 5: FOCUS

What we focus on determines our reality. When we experience anxiety, it's usually because we're doing what's called *stacking*. We're stacking a bunch of fears, worries, insecurities, and stresses on top of each other. As things happen all around us during a typical day, we stack them on top of each other. As a result, we can't focus very well on any one thing. When our stack turns into one big problem, it becomes too heavy a burden to bear. We find it hard to focus on anything else—even on the good things happening in our lives.

Focus Exercise

To illustrate how we can improve our focus, I'm going to give you a little exercise. For a second, look around the room. If you're outside, look at your surroundings. See if you can spot anything blue. Just stuff that's blue. Now, close your eyes, and name all the things you saw that were red. Tough, huh? You might be able to list one or two red things, but you're probably not going to remember many. That doesn't mean red things weren't there, and it doesn't mean you saw only blue stuff. You didn't see much red because you weren't looking for it.

When you're focused, your mental state is consumed entirely with that one thing you're focused on. This exercise illustrates that when we have one thing on our mind, it's hard to notice anything else. Now I'm going to show you how to change your focus so you can instantly reduce stress and anxiety.

Strategy 1: What-if Discrimination

A lot of anxiety stems from the phrase "what if." Anxiety comes from perpetual and excessive worry. When you worry about something or several things for an extended period, you create anxiety. When you use the phrase "what if," most of the time you're relating the phrase to something negative. I call this "what-if discrimination." You're discriminating against the positive possibilities in life. It's easy to discriminate against the positive because your brain is trying to keep you alive and neutralize threats. That voice in your head gives you the worst-case scenario immediately.

Well, what if you say the wrong thing? What if you do something wrong? What if your boss isn't happy with you? What if your spouse doesn't like it? What if, what if, what if. Well, what if you say the right thing? What if you do the right thing? What if your boss promotes you? What if your spouse loves it? We never think about that. We think only about the negative side because our brain is trying to stop potential suffering. What's funny is that in an effort to stop potential suffering, our brains create immediate suffering in the moment. It's called anxiety.

So, stop your what-if discrimination. Any time that voice in your head says, "What if such and such negative thing happens," think of the opposite possibility. Don't discriminate. Focus on the upside.

Strategy 2: See the Good

To change your focus, learn to ask yourself better questions. I used this technique in Chapter 1. You need to see the good in life so that you can maintain a mental state of optimism. When you start to feel overwhelmed or anxious, ask yourself the following questions:

1. How can this benefit me?
2. What's good about this?

3. How can I make the best of this?
4. What can I do differently next time?
5. What can I learn from this?

To give you an example, let's say I have no money in my bank savings account, and it's stressing me out. On top of other things weighing me down, not having money really hurts. Let's run through the questions above and how to answer them.

1. How can this benefit me? Rationing my food will help me to finally go through that mess in the pantry. I can clean it up and organize it in the process.
2. What's good about this? In the future, I'll be able to relate to anyone with money troubles and make an effort to help those people. I'll be able to speak from personal experience.
3. How can I make the best of this? Maybe I could ask a friend or a parent if they have any work I could do for them to earn some quick cash.
4. What can I do differently next time? This shortfall gives me an opportunity to budget better next month. I didn't expect to get a flat tire, and that threw me off. Maybe I could set aside a small amount of money each month for an emergency fund so it doesn't happen again.
5. What can I learn from this? Life has its ups and downs. I need to come up with ways to be better prepared during the ups to ensure success during the downs.

When you change your focus, you start to see your challenges as stepping stones to success. Your mental state changes from pessimism to optimism. Start to ask yourself better questions, and you'll begin to transform from anxious to awesome.

Strategy 3: Visualization

The last strategy to use every day is to perform a visualization technique. Before I discovered for myself the benefits of visualization, I was extremely skeptical of it. I thought that visualization—forming mental images to influence our bodies and minds to better reach our full potential—was ridiculous and that it wouldn't benefit me to sit in a room and do nothing physical. I remember thinking, *No, meditation is for hippies and "ultra-spiritual" people. It's weird.* But once I willingly embraced it, I saw the impact immediately. I couldn't believe I had been so wrong about it. Don't let previous experience or biases stop you from doing this.

I mentioned the Tony Robbins priming exercise in Chapter 4. It involves your physiology. Tony asks you to put your hands above your head, bring them down, and then breathe in and out of your nose quickly. If you didn't look it up on YouTube while reading Chapter 4, do it now! To help me focus, I close my eyes and put on my headphones. Performing a visualization technique every day will help you focus on the day—and life—you want to create. Priming also helps you get into a mental state of gratitude. You need to connect with those mental states every single day. I recommend doing priming first thing in the morning. It takes about 15 minutes. Make it part of your regular routine.

6

MORNING PEOPLE

"I'm going to do it!" I told myself. "I'm going to start waking up early." It was past time for me to be productive in the morning. So, I set my alarm for 6:00 a.m., which was two hours earlier than I normally rolled out of bed. But the next morning at 6:00 a.m., my hand couldn't even make it to the alarm clock before the voices in my head delivered their usual package of excuses: "It's too dark. It's too cold. It's too early. You went to bed late. You can start tomorrow." And so on.

Those excuses gave me permission to hit the snooze button and go back to sleep, feeling completely justified. If anyone thought otherwise, I'd give them a piece of my mind. The voices continued: "Getting up at 6:00 a.m. is for *morning people,* not me. I don't want to exercise anyway. Besides, I'll be tired the rest of the day if I get up early. If I were a morning person, it would be easier. But I'm not, so I'll go back to sleep." I reached over and turned off the alarm.

TOOL 6: ENVIRONMENT

Tool 6 is all about using your environment to support you. We have only so much willpower to withstand stress and overwhelmed feelings. So, what I had to do was use my environment to support my goal. Here's what I did to get up early in the morning:

- I moved the alarm clock away from my bed so I had to get up to turn it off.
- I opened my blinds; natural light helps to transition out of deep sleep. (Or I could have bought a light-therapy alarm clock that simulates a sunrise.)
- I turned up the thermostat; if my house is warm, I'm more likely to get up.

Your Space

You may be adding to your anxiety each day through your environment. In my story, my mind used my environment against me. It was too dark, it was too cold, it was too easy to turn off the alarm, and so forth. We need to turn the tables and create environments that promote peace and relief from stress. Some people have stress balls on their desk at work, but their desk is a complete mess, which causes stress.

To get rid of anxiety, you should set up an environment that promotes feelings of joy and peace. Clutter creates stress, so put things away. Do you live in a basement room with no natural light? Get some natural-light lamps to brighten things up. Buy a plant or two, and make your space feel more natural. A space that's clean, organized, and bright can help keep you from feeling overwhelmed.

Think about the spaces you occupy in a day. What do they look like right now? Clean and organize the following areas:

- Bedroom
- Bathroom
- Kitchen
- Car
- Work space

Set aside an hour every week to check each of these spaces for trash, disorganization, and clutter. If you find anything out of order, clean it up. Any time I visit a client in a dirty home, I think, "This place is giving me anxiety, and I don't even live here."

Your People

Another part of our environment is people. I like to include people in the environment tool even though we can't really control them. "Our" people include our friends, our family, our coworkers, and our boss, among others. People are part of our lives every single day. When we're trying to make a life change to get rid of anxiety, we're going to find that people fit in one of two categories.

1. Supporters

Supporters are people who are encouraging, helpful, and uplifting. They're people you like to spend time with because they have an optimistic view on life. They're motivated, and they help motivate you. They want to see you succeed. They give you good feedback, they believe in you, and sometimes they want to join you. They say things like, "Hey, I want to be part of this. This is awesome! How can I help?"

2. Doubters

Doubters, the other category, are hard to avoid. That's because we may relate to them directly. If we feel that life has handed us a bad hand and that we are destined to suffer, for example, we naturally gravitate toward people who also feel that way. We go to lunch with them and talk about how crappy our lives are. Doubters say things like, "You're trying to get rid of anxiety? Well, good luck, dude. Anxiety is just part of our genetics. Getting rid of it is not going to happen. There's nothing you can do about it. I've tried this exact same thing you're doing. It doesn't work."

Just because something didn't work for others doesn't mean it's not going to work for you. They likely never believed it was going to work in the first place. We *must* first believe before we can give something our best shot. Doubt can become a self-fulfilling prophecy. So, don't give too much credit to the doubters. Instead, surround yourself with supporters.

This is a tough part of the environment tool because you may need to change your social circles. If you spend your time with doubters, you will find it extremely tough to make a change. Find supporters and spend time with them. I can provide coaching, and I can help you find others on the same journey as you. Visit chrisdinehart.com for details.

Anybody can be a doubter or a supporter—from therapists and doctors to parents, siblings, and friends. Doubters will undermine your determination with their doubts. They will make you feel dumb for trying to get rid of anxiety, for standing up and celebrating, for putting your hands above your head. They'll be critical of every tool you've received. They'll say things like, "You look ridiculous. That's stupid. How could that possibly do anything for you?"

Ironically, doubters usually have the best of intentions. They think they're protecting you or helping you to avoid pain that they or someone they knew experienced. They're not you, though. They don't know that you have the tools and strategies you need. I faced plenty of doubters when I was trying to make changes, but now those doubters ask me how I did it. They want to know how I made it happen. This book is my answer.

Your Time

As with any change, time is a big factor. If you want to get rid of your anxiety, you've got to dedicate time to do it. But it doesn't have to be a lot of time. I didn't dedicate a lot of time, because I still have a job and I still have a family. I'm still a father, I'm still a husband, I'm still a brother, I'm still an uncle. Change can come as fast or as slow as you're willing to make things happen. I can tell you from personal experience that over time, my thinking has completely changed.

The REAL me!

CONCLUSION

To conclude, let's review the six important tools I've shared in this book.

1. The Secret

Remember, the secret to eliminating anxiety lies in what you believe is possible. When you believe in a better version of yourself, you open the door to becoming that better version. Belief comes before everything else. It makes everything else possible.

We build beliefs by going through the belief cycle. Our thoughts lead to action, action leads to results, and results lead to beliefs. When we question our limiting beliefs, envision new beliefs, and then reinforce those new beliefs, we start to create a fundamental shift in our thinking. We create change. Change your thoughts about anxiety, change the action you take, and then change the meaning of the results so that you replace discouraging beliefs with empowering beliefs.

You are more than what you have become. It's time to believe in yourself. Believe in a better future. Believe in a better life. Believe in a better version of you. As my favorite song from the band Journey says, "Don't stop believing!"

2. Real Decisions

Don't forget about the power of a real decision. Hernán Cortés knew how powerful a committed decision could be. Because of his resolve, it's impossible to visit Mexico and Central America today without seeing the influence of the Spanish conquistador. The Spanish influence is reflected in the language, governments, architecture, culture, and much more.

You won't know what type of impact you could have if you don't decide to implement what you've learned in this book. You've got to decide that your only option is to rid yourself of your anxiety. Decide to eliminate the anxiety in your life, and you will have a massive impact on countless others. This victory will positively affect your relationships, career, physical health, and overall quality of life. It's all up to you, so decide now because destiny waits for no one.

3. Pain and Pleasure

Pain and pleasure drive us to do almost everything we do in life. Our brains have evolved over time to associate pain with some things and pleasure with others. Anxiety is a form of pain that I had associated with social interactions and public speaking. When my constant worry spiraled out of control, it often caused more anxiety. But when I learned how to break down and eliminate false connections, my life changed forever.

You too can learn to create new connections and eliminate old ones. Reprogramming your mind takes concentrated and intentional effort, but with persistence, you will become a different person. When you create better connections, you think differently. Make pain and pleasure work for you rather than control you.

4. Physiology

How you feel right now is the quality of life that you're experiencing. If you want a higher quality of life, change how you feel. You can change how you feel in an instant by changing your physiology. You'll feel different, for example, if you put this book down and jump up and down as if you had just won the lottery. It doesn't matter if you actually got any money. Celebration is a powerful tool.

You can also use cold plunges to change the way you feel. Conquering something uncomfortable every morning will get you a little win to start the day. Use music and dance. Move your body. Use breathing techniques to change your state of mind to feel calmer and more balanced. Use power poses and movements each day. Your body can be a powerful tool to get rid of anxiety in an instant if you use it properly.

And don't forget about the high fives. The high-five challenge will bring energy and optimism to your life if you give everyone in sight a high five.

5. Focus

Stop discriminating. "What-if discrimination" leads to more worry and anxiousness. We tend to get more and more creative with negative possibilities when we discriminate against the positive. "What-if discrimination" will rob us of the ability to see the good in the world. Let's flip the script and use focus to think about the positive. What if things go right? What if everything turns out better than we expected?

You will get in life what you focus on. Don't focus on the obstacles in the river of life, focus on the goal. Focus all your time and energy getting to where you want to go, and don't waste time and energy on the rest. When you focus on the positive and ask yourself the right questions, the negative things in life don't seem so big. Remember to ask yourself, "How can this benefit me?" This is how you can use focus to get rid of anxiety in an instant.

6. Environment

Your environment could be contributing to your struggle because it supports the type of lifestyle you currently live. Think about what part of your environment needs to change so you can get rid of anxiety. Do you need to clean your car, home, or workspace to create less clutter and less stress? Do you need to open the blinds or get a sunrise clock so you can introduce more natural light into your life? Do you consume entertainment that creates fear? If the answer to these questions is yes, then taking action to make changes will have a big impact on your ability to take control of your thinking. It's extremely difficult to withstand the temptation of returning to our old habits, but if our new environment eliminates the temptation altogether, we won't have to withstand anything.

Your environment includes your social circles. Who in your life is a doubter and who is a supporter? What can you do differently to eliminate or better handle the relationships you have with doubters? Don't let the doubters choose your path for you. Don't let them discourage you from your goal. They're not you. They don't have the tools you now have. They don't believe. Give yourself some grace and time to make changes. Don't let the doubters stop you.

The life you're trying to create is not just possible; it's actually waiting for you. It's real. When I got rid of anxiety, I felt like I was finally the real me. Today, I don't recognize the person I was for 20 years. I don't know who that guy was, but I know he was definitely not the real me—the me I've always wanted to be, the me who is confident, excited, and full of love and life. I finally got to become that guy.

I always knew deep down that I was more than this thing, this anxiety, that was happening to me. I always knew that there was something greater out there for me. Likewise, you deserve more than what you're getting out of life right now. You know it. If you search your heart deep enough, you know that there's more out there for you. So, start today. It's time to *live for more.*

ACKNOWLEDGMENTS

I don't have enough pages to thank everyone. This book is a culmination of life experiences and helping hands along the way. Thanks to:

My wife, Emily, for your relentless support and love. You are always willing to bet on me, even when it appears that the odds are stacked against me.

My children, Justin, Lily, and Maddy, for bringing joy to my life every day. It's an honor to be your father.

My father, Justin, for always showing me strength. I owe my drive and determination to your example of what a father and husband should be.

My mother, AnnaLisa, for always making me feel loved. Your love and care for me got me through some of the toughest times of my life.

The Morris family—Michael Sr. (my editor), Susan, Chris, James, Michael Jr., Michelle, Sam, Rachel, and Tom—for accepting me into your family and supporting me. Each of you has something unique and powerful that you bring to the family, and it's an honor to be part of it.

Friends at NorthStar home—Adam Bailey, Jason Christensen, and Danielle Lewis—for your willingness to believe and bet on me, which created an incredible transformation in my life. None of this would have been possible without you.

Tony Robbins, whose "Unleash the Power Within" personal development seminar inspired me to follow my heart and never give up. Your selfless service and genuine love shocked me into believing in myself.

Dean Graziosi, for bringing energy and optimism to my life every day. The KBB has made an incredible impact on my life, and your *Millionaire Success Habits* helped me change my lifestyle for the better.

Russell Brunson, for the One Funnel Away Challenge. I always wanted to write a book, and you got me to sit down and work for hours and hours on it until I finished. Your energy is contagious and inspiring.

Finally, thanks to Joshua T. Dennis for his amazing design and David A. Green for his awesome illustrations.

— Notes —

— Notes —

— Notes —

— Notes —

ABOUT THE AUTHOR

Chris Dinehart grew up in Provo, Utah. He served a Church service mission in Queztaltenango, Guatemala, and now lives in Utah with his wife and children.

In addition to being a certified strategic life coach, he has master practitioner certifications in neuro-linguistic programming and cognitive behavioral theory. He has personally coached hundreds of individuals, including athletes from Division I collegiate sports and the PGA Tour Champions.

To learn more about Chris's work, visit chrisdinehart.com.

Scan to visit

chrisdinehart.com